T0361549

Who Was
Frederick
Douglass?

Who Was Frederick Douglass?

by April Jones Prince

illustrated by Robert Squier

Penguin Workshop

For my extraordinary parents—Bill and Carol Jones—whose
energy and creativity inspire me every day—AJP

For my wife, Jessica. I couldn't ask for a better friend—or
research assistant—RS

PENGUIN WORKSHOP
An Imprint of Penguin Random House LLC, New York

If you purchased this book without a cover, you should be aware that this book is stolen
property. It was reported as "unsold and destroyed" to the publisher, and neither the author
nor the publisher has received any payment for this "stripped book."

Visit us online at www.penguinrandomhouse.com.

Library of Congress Control Number: 2014039149

ISBN 9780448479118   20 19 18 17

Contents

Who Was
Frederick Douglass?

Frederick Douglass was born enslaved. Just like a horse or a plow, he was the property of a white man. From a young age, Frederick wondered why that was so. Wasn't he as smart, strong, and deserving of liberty as anyone else?

At the time Frederick was born, in 1818, there

were 1.5 million enslaved people in the southern United States. Most didn't learn to read. This was against the law! But Frederick taught himself to read and write.

Most enslaved people didn't risk their lives to run away to freedom. This was against the law, too. But Frederick escaped and helped others do the same.

Most enslaved people who escaped to freedom did not speak out against slavery, because they

feared they would be recaptured. It was very dangerous to do so. But Frederick spoke up anyway. With words as his weapons, Frederick spent his life fighting for equal rights for all people. He was the father of the civil rights movement.

Chapter 1
Born into Slavery

The man who became famous as Frederick Douglass was born in a log hut on the eastern shore of Maryland in 1818. His name at birth was Frederick Augustus Washington Bailey.

Frederick's mother, Harriet, was enslaved, which meant Frederick was, too. They were enslaved by a man named Aaron Anthony. They called him Captain Anthony or "Old Master."

Who was Frederick's father? It may have been Captain Anthony. Frederick never knew for sure.

Captain Anthony owned three farms and enslaved about thirty people. He also managed the farms of a very rich man named Edward Lloyd. The Lloyd family owned thirteen farms and enslaved more than five hundred. Captain Anthony lived on the Lloyds' main farm, Wye House plantation. Some of the people Captain Anthony enslaved lived there with him. Others, including members of Frederick's family, were spread out across other farms.

Frederick's mother worked long hours in Captain Anthony's fields or in those of a neighbor who rented her. Frederick saw his mother only four or five times in his life. Instead, he lived with his grandparents, Isaac and Betsey Bailey. Isaac was a free Black man, but Betsey was enslaved. Her job was to care for her many young grandchildren until they were old enough to work.

As a child, Frederick enjoyed fishing in a
nearby stream and watching squirrels scamper
about. His grandparents' windowless cabin, with
its clay floor and dirt-and-straw chimney, was
small and rough. But to Frederick, it held "the
attractions of a palace."

Then one day Betsey brought him to work at Captain Anthony's. Betsey kept the reason for their journey a secret so as not to upset young Frederick. It was a twelve-mile walk, so his strong grandmother had to "tote" him on her shoulders now and then.

In the heat of the afternoon, they finally arrived at the grandest building Frederick had ever seen. Wye House was white, with stately pillars and a neatly trimmed lawn. The plantation sat on the Wye River and was like its own little village, with barns, stables, kitchens, blacksmith's and shoemaker's shops, and more. Captain Anthony lived in a separate house on the property.

SLAVERY IN AMERICA

SLAVERY HAD BEEN PART OF AMERICAN HISTORY SINCE EARLY COLONIAL DAYS. THE FIRST AFRICANS WERE KIDNAPPED FROM THEIR HOMELANDS IN WEST AFRICA AND BROUGHT TO VIRGINIA BY SHIP IN 1619. THE TRADING OF ENSLAVED PEOPLE CONTINUED FOR ALMOST TWO HUNDRED YEARS, UNTIL IT WAS OUTLAWED IN 1808. NO NEW KIDNAPPED AFRICANS COULD BE BROUGHT INTO THE COUNTRY AFTER THIS TIME, BUT EXISTING ENSLAVED PEOPLE HAD CHILDREN. BY 1860, THERE WERE FOUR MILLION ENSLAVED PEOPLE IN THE SOUTHERN STATES, WHERE LARGE WHEAT, COTTON, TOBACCO, SUGAR, AND RICE PLANTATIONS DEPENDED ON THE LABOR OF ENSLAVED PEOPLE. IN THE NORTH, WHERE FARMS WERE SMALLER, SLAVERY WAS NOT AS COMMON OR AS PROFITABLE. FOR THIS AND OTHER REASONS, SLAVERY IN THE NORTH GRADUALLY DIED OUT.

Energetic enslaved children surrounded Frederick when he arrived at Wye House. Frederick's grandmother introduced him to his brother and two sisters, whom he'd never met. Betsey encouraged Frederick to play with the children, and he finally, reluctantly, joined them. Sometime later, one of them ran up and hollered, "Fed, Fed! Grandmammy gone!" Frederick raced to the kitchen to see for himself. Betsey was indeed gone, for good. "Almost heart-broken at the discovery," Frederick later wrote, "I fell upon the ground, and wept a boy's bitter tears." It was the first time he experienced the cruelty of slavery.

One morning soon after, Frederick was sleeping in a rough kitchen closet. Suddenly he woke to the terrible shrieks of his aunt Hester. Captain Anthony was whipping Hester for spending time with her boyfriend.

Frederick watched through cracks in the closet door. He never forgot the horrific scene. From that day on, Frederick hated slavery with all his heart and soul.

Because Frederick was still too young to work in the fields, he ran errands, looked after the cows and chickens, and kept the front yard clean. It wasn't hard labor—not anything like hoeing, planting, weeding, and harvesting crops from sunup to sundown. He wasn't often whipped or beaten, but he was cold and hungry. "In hottest summer and coldest winter," Frederick remembered, "I was kept almost naked—no shoes, no stockings, no jacket, no trousers, nothing on but a coarse tow linen shirt, reaching only to my knees." Frederick slept on the dirt floor of the kitchen closet, without a bed or blanket. On the coldest nights, he'd climb inside a corn sack to try to keep warm.

The hunger was even worse. "Aunt" Katy was a coldhearted enslaved woman who looked after the enslaved children. She served cornmeal mush in a long trough placed on the ground. The strongest children got the most food, but even that wasn't much.

Sometimes Frederick's belly was so empty, he fought the dog for crumbs that fell from the table where Aunt Katy prepared food for Captain Anthony's family.

One day, Aunt Katy made Frederick go the

whole day without food. That night, he quietly plucked a few grains from an ear of Indian corn. He was roasting the grains by the fire when his mother appeared on one of her few visits. Harriet was furious when she learned that her son had not eaten. She gave Aunt Katy a fiery lecture and replaced Frederick's corn with a heart-shaped ginger cake. In the care of his mother, Frederick felt like a king. But when morning came, his mother was gone. He never saw her again. Harriet died shortly thereafter, though no one bothered to tell Frederick until sometime later.

Thankfully, better days were ahead.

Chapter 2
Baltimore

At Wye House, Frederick ran errands for Miss Lucretia, Captain Anthony's daughter. Sometimes, when Frederick was especially hungry, he would stand beneath Miss Lucretia's window and sing.

CAPTAIN
THOMAS AULD

Miss Lucretia often rewarded him with a piece of bread. This small act of kindness was like a sunbeam in young Frederick's life.

Frederick had been at Wye House about two years when Miss Lucretia and her husband, Thomas Auld, sent Frederick off to Baltimore, Maryland. Frederick would live with Thomas's brother Hugh Auld and his wife, Sophia. It would be Frederick's job to run errands and look after the couple's two-year-old son, Tommy. Frederick was thrilled. He was only eight, but he was bright and curious. He had always wondered about life in the big city.

Before leaving, Frederick spent the better part of three days in the creek, scrubbing. Miss Lucretia gave him his first pair of pants.

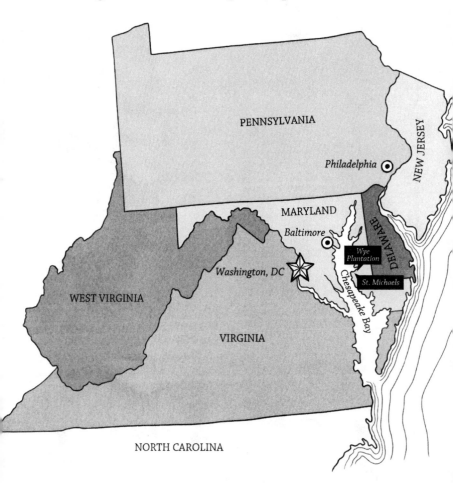

On a Saturday morning, Frederick boarded a boat at the Wye House wharf, hoping never to see the plantation again.

For a boy who had always lived in the country, the city of Baltimore was overwhelming. With more than sixty thousand residents, Baltimore was one of the largest cities in the United States. Tall brick buildings shut out the sky. Delivery wagons crowded the busy streets as they headed to and from the harbor. The sun beat down on the hard brick pavements, almost blistering Frederick's bare feet.

A ship's hand brought Frederick to his new
home. The Auld family met Frederick at the door.
Frederick loved little Tommy at once, and he was
surprised by the kind look on Sophia Auld's face.
Mrs. Auld had never enslaved someone before,
and she treated Frederick more like a son. For the
first time in his life, Frederick slept in a bed with
covers. He had good bread to eat and clean clothes
to wear.

He also discovered there were such things as books. He asked his mistress to teach him to read. And she did. In no time, Frederick had learned the alphabet and could spell short words. Proud of his progress, Sophia told her husband about it.

Hugh Auld's response was swift and sure. He forbade his wife to teach Frederick anymore. Not only was it against the law, he said, but an education would make an enslaved person want to escape.

Mr. Auld was right. Frederick understood that knowledge was power. "From that moment," Frederick said, "I understood the pathway from slavery to freedom."

From then on, whenever Frederick ran an errand, he carried a book and pieces of bread. He would do his errand quickly, then find a hungry white boy in the streets and trade bread for a lesson.

When Frederick was twelve, he bought his first book with fifty cents he had earned shining shoes in the street. *The Columbian Orator* was filled with speeches by famous people. One was a discussion between an enslaver and an enslaved person, in which the enslaved person stated the many reasons why slavery was wrong. His points were so strong, the enslaver unexpectedly set him free. Frederick read this speech over and over. For him, however, freedom seemed to be forever out of reach.

At the Aulds' house, Frederick began to hear the word *abolition*. He didn't know what this word meant. Hugh Auld and his friends would bring it up when they were discussing slavery. A dictionary told Frederick that *abolition* meant "the act of ending something." Then in a newspaper, he found an article about the abolition of slavery. There were people—abolitionists—who wanted slavery to end. There were groups of abolitionists in Northern states trying to help enslaved people escape to freedom. This was astounding news.

Frederick began thinking about how to run away to the North. He was around thirteen, too young to plan an escape. But the thought gave him hope. Also, before he escaped, there was something important Frederick wanted to do: learn to write. With this ability, he might be able to write a fake permission slip from the person who was enslaving him, allowing him to travel north safely. Frederick practiced writing, using chalk on fences and pavement.

Later, Frederick copied letters in Tommy's old spelling book. Sometimes he worked late into the night after the family had gone to bed. It took years of hard work, but finally he learned to write.

Chapter 3
Becoming a Man

While Frederick was in Baltimore, Captain Anthony died. This meant Frederick was now the property of Miss Lucretia and her husband, Thomas. It wasn't long before Lucretia died, too.

When Frederick was fifteen, Hugh and Thomas Auld had an argument. Thomas demanded that Frederick be sent to him where he was now living, in the run-down port of Saint Michaels, near Frederick's birthplace.

This was bad news for Frederick. Thomas Auld was stingy.

Frederick and the other enslaved people had to beg and steal for food, while bread and meat sat spoiling in Thomas's storehouses.

Frederick sometimes let Mr. Auld's horse run off just so he could go after it. The horse liked the neighbor's pasture, and Frederick liked the bread he got from the cook there.

Thomas Auld knew what Frederick was doing and decided that city life had "ruined" Frederick. He was "spoiled."

To make Frederick more obedient, Thomas hired him out to a brutal enslaver named Edward Covey. Mr. Covey rented a farm seven miles away on Chesapeake Bay.

Mr. Covey made Frederick and the others work in the fields in all weather, sometimes until midnight.

"It was never too hot or too cold; it could never rain, blow, hail, or snow too hard for us to work in the field," Frederick remembered.

One blazing August day, Frederick and a few
others were separating wheat from straw. Suddenly
Frederick, dizzy and shaking, collapsed from
the heat and hard work. Covey kicked him and
told him to get up. When Frederick couldn't,
Covey hit him over the head with a slat of wood.
Blood ran freely from Frederick's head as Covey
continued to kick him and shout. Finally, Covey
left Frederick lying in the dirt.

Not long after, Frederick was tending the horses when he felt a rope slip around his ankles. Covey meant to take him down. But something in Frederick snapped. He had been worked like an animal long enough! Frederick grabbed Covey's throat and didn't let go. It was rare—and dangerous—for an enslaved person to attack a white man.

After nearly two hours of fighting, Covey gave up. He never laid a hand on Frederick again.

The fight with Covey was a turning point in Frederick's life as an enslaved person. "I was nothing before; I was a man now," Frederick later wrote. His desire to be free grew stronger than ever.

When Frederick's year with Covey was up, he was sent to work at the nearby farm of William Freeland. Mr. Freeland worked his people hard, but not past sundown. He didn't whip them. He provided good tools to work with and enough food to eat.

Frederick made some of the best friends of his life at Mr. Freeland's. Before long, he was spending his Sundays and three nights a week teaching them to read in secret. Though they risked forty lashes

on their bare backs for doing this, Frederick's school grew to include more than forty eager students.

By the time he was eighteen, Frederick decided to make plans to escape. Not wanting to leave his good friends behind, he shared his ideas about escaping to freedom. Four friends agreed to come with him. On Easter weekend, they planned to steal a canoe and paddle up Chesapeake Bay about seventy miles, then follow the North Star on foot until they reached a free state. Frederick wrote out fake passes for himself and his friends, giving them all permission to visit Baltimore.

Frederick signed the passes from "William Hamilton," who enslaved one of his friends.

Easter Saturday arrived. Early in the morning, the men went to the fields as usual. Frederick had the strange feeling that someone had given them away. Sure enough, four white men arrived on horseback. They tied up the five suspects and dragged them fifteen miles to jail.

The only proof of the friend's plan was the passes Frederick had written. He had quietly thrown his into the fire before he was taken away. He whispered to the others to eat theirs with their morning biscuits.

After the Easter holidays, Frederick's friends were released from jail by the people who were enslaving them and taken home. Frederick remained in jail another week, but then he got a lucky break. Thomas arrived. He was sending Frederick back to his brother Hugh in Baltimore. Thomas said that if Frederick learned a trade and behaved himself, he would free him at age twenty-five. "The promise had but one fault," Frederick later wrote. "It seemed too good to be true."

Chapter 4
Escape!

Frederick was now six feet tall, strong, and smart. Hugh hired him out to one of the many shipyards in Baltimore. Frederick was to do whatever jobs were needed. "Fred, bring that roller here!—Fred, go get a fresh can of water.—Fred, come help saw off the end of this timber." For eight months, Frederick worked alongside free Black and white people. At another shipyard, Frederick

learned to caulk, or fill the cracks in a ship's hull so it wouldn't leak. Within a year, Frederick was earning as much as nine dollars a week. All this money went to Hugh. Frederick felt he was being robbed of his own wages. Hugh hadn't earned the money. Why should he get to keep it? The reason was slavery. And the only answer was to once again plan an escape.

Frederick needed to set some money aside for himself. He convinced Hugh to let him find his own work. Frederick would buy his own food and tools and pay for a place to live. All these expenses would cost about six dollars a week. Hugh wouldn't have to pay for any of them.

In addition, every Saturday Frederick would give Hugh three dollars. This was a good deal for Hugh, who didn't have to support Frederick any longer. But it was hard for Frederick, who would have to caulk six days a week and pick up other jobs, too. Still, he was up for the challenge

and managed to put away a little of the money
each week.

During this time
Frederick met a free Black
woman named Anna
Murray. Anna worked
as a housekeeper for
a rich white family.
She and Frederick
fell in love and
hoped to marry.

One weekend in
August, Frederick
was late bringing Hugh

ANNA MURRAY

Auld his three dollars. Angry, Hugh stopped
letting Frederick hire himself out for jobs.
Frederick went back to living with Hugh.
This was something he could not endure.

With the money he had saved, and more from
Anna, he would make a run for the North. He set
a date he would leave: September 3, 1838. Anna
would follow later.

As the date approached, Frederick grew uneasy. If he were caught again, he would surely be sold farther south. There, it would be much harder to escape, because the distance to any free state would be so much longer. Anna carefully tailored Frederick's clothing to look like the uniform of a sailor.

On Monday morning, Frederick left the Auld house for work, as usual. But instead of going to the shipyard, Frederick boarded a northbound train from Baltimore. He wore a red shirt, a black tie knotted loosely around his neck, and a broad-

brimmed sailor's hat. As proof of his freedom, he carried a friend's seaman's papers. These papers described Frederick's friend—who had much darker skin than Frederick. If anyone looked closely and discovered this, Frederick would be arrested.

On the train, the conductor asked Frederick for his free papers. "My whole future depended upon the decision of this conductor," Frederick knew. Satisfied by the American eagle on top of the seaman's papers, the conductor looked no further.

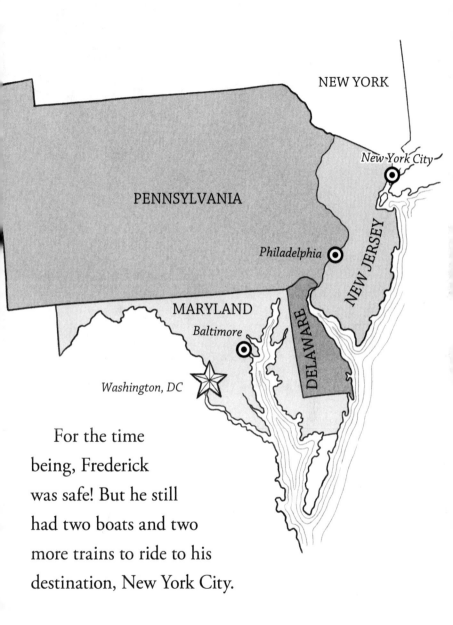

NEW YORK

New York City

PENNSYLVANIA

Philadelphia

NEW JERSEY

MARYLAND

DELAWARE

Baltimore

Washington, DC

For the time
being, Frederick
was safe! But he still
had two boats and two
more trains to ride to his
destination, New York City.

Finally, Frederick arrived in New York. "My chains were broken," he said. "I was a FREEMAN." Describing his excitement to a friend, he wrote, "I felt as one might feel upon escape from a den of hungry lions."

The sights of New York dazzled Frederick. But

he realized he had to be careful. People who were hired to search for and recapture enslaved people kept close watch everywhere enslaved people who were seeking freedom were likely to go for help or shelter. Anyone might turn him in for a few dollars. If that happened, he would be sent back to Hugh. "I was afraid to speak to any one for fear of speaking to the wrong one," Frederick said. He wandered the streets of New York and slept at least one night among barrels on the wharves. "I was indeed free—from slavery," Frederick later wrote, "but free from food and shelter as well."

Finally, Frederick shared his story with an honest-looking sailor, who took him to the home of David Ruggles. Mr. Ruggles was a Black abolitionist who helped freedom seekers.

DAVID RUGGLES

Mr. Ruggles hid Frederick in his home for several days. Frederick sent for Anna, who arrived shortly. The two were married on September 15, 1838.

Mr. Ruggles decided the best place for Frederick to go to find work was New Bedford, Massachusetts. Many ships were repaired and outfitted on the wharves there. The growing city had a large community of formerly enslaved people, who looked out for one another. The hired searchers knew better than to come there, or they would be run out of town.

After Frederick and Anna's wedding ceremony, the couple boarded a steamboat and set out on their new life together. No matter what hardships might lie ahead, now the future held hope.

Chapter 5
Life in the North

When Frederick and Anna arrived in New Bedford, a free Black couple named Mary and Nathan Johnson helped them get started. While in New York, Frederick had given up the last name Bailey in case the Aulds came looking for him. He took the name Johnson instead. But in New Bedford, there were already so many Johnsons. It was easy to confuse them! Nathan Johnson suggested the new last name Douglas, after a character in a poem he was reading. Frederick agreed but added an extra *s* at the end.

Eager to find work, Frederick went to the wharves. The scene was quite different from the shipyards in Baltimore. Here the workers were

quiet, focused, and cheerful. There was
no whipping, no yelling of mean
names, no loud songs.

The white caulkers refused to work with a
Black man, so Frederick's first job was stocking a
ship with oil. "It was new, hard, and dirty work,"
he wrote, "but I went at it with a glad heart and
a willing hand. I was now my own master."

Soon he and Anna had their first daughter, Rosetta. Four more children would follow: Lewis, Frederick Jr., Charles, and Annie.

In New Bedford, Frederick began reading a newspaper called *The Liberator*. Published by William Lloyd Garrison, the paper spoke out fiercely against slavery. "The paper became my meat and my drink," Frederick said. Reading the paper inspired him to go to antislavery meetings. He listened, and he spoke about the evils of

slavery to his friends and members of the Black church he and Anna had joined.

In 1841, Frederick attended a meeting of the American Anti-Slavery Society. He was asked if he would say a few words about his experience with slavery. There were hundreds, maybe a thousand people, in the audience. "I trembled in every limb," he remembered.

WILLIAM LLOYD GARRISON

BORN IN 1805 IN
NEWBURYPORT, MASSACHUSETTS,
WILLIAM LLOYD GARRISON WAS
ONE OF THE MOST PASSIONATE
AND FAMOUS LEADERS OF
THE ANTISLAVERY MOVEMENT.
IN 1831, HE BEGAN PUBLISHING
THE LIBERATOR, A WEEKLY
NEWSPAPER. IN THE FIRST
EDITION, HE WROTE, "I DO
NOT WISH TO THINK, OR
SPEAK, OR WRITE, WITH MODERATION. . . .
I AM IN EARNEST—I WILL NOT EQUIVOCATE—
I WILL NOT EXCUSE—I WILL NOT RETREAT A
SINGLE INCH—AND I WILL BE HEARD." GARRISON
PUBLISHED THE PAPER FOR THIRTY-FIVE YEARS,
NEVER MISSING AN ISSUE.

GARRISON DID NOT BELIEVE IN VIOLENCE
TO ACHIEVE HIS GOALS. INSTEAD, HE RELIED
ON WRITING AND SPEAKING OUT ABOUT THE
EVILS OF SLAVERY TO PERSUADE AMERICANS
TO END THE PRACTICE. GARRISON WAS ALSO A
STRONG SUPPORTER OF WOMEN'S RIGHTS AND
WAS COMMITTED TO THAT CAUSE UNTIL HE DIED
IN 1879.

Later Frederick recalled little of what he said. But he remembered the excitement of the audience. White people in the North had never heard a formerly enslaved person speak about the terrible life of slavery. Frederick's story was powerful.

After the meeting, the Anti-Slavery Society offered Frederick work as a speaker. Frederick didn't think he could do a good job. More important, speaking out might help the Aulds find and capture him. But the Society kept asking. And Frederick agreed to try.

For four years, Frederick traveled across New England, then south and west to New York, Ohio, Indiana, and Pennsylvania. With his deep voice, sharp eyes, tall form, and passionate words, he told Americans about his childhood in slavery. He was serious but also smart, touching, and funny. Large crowds came to hear him in parks, halls, churches, and schoolhouses. He could make them laugh and cry.

Speaking up took real courage. Some didn't welcome his message. They yelled insults and threw bricks, rotten eggs, or vegetables at him. In one town in Indiana, Frederick was attacked by a mob and had his hand broken. But Frederick pressed on, feeling that if people knew the brutal nature of slavery as he did, they would rush to end it. To avoid being captured, Frederick was careful never to give his real name, the names of the people who enslaved him, or the places he had lived.

At first he was content to describe his experiences in slavery. After months of telling the same story, he began not only describing slavery but speaking out against it.

He also talked about the poor treatment of Black people in the North. Often, hotels and restaurants would not serve him. On trains, he had to sit in the dirty, uncomfortable "colored" car. (The word *colored* was once used to describe Black people, but it is now considered offensive.) Once, he paid for a first-class ticket and refused to leave the "whites-only" section. The conductor called several brakemen to remove him, but Frederick held tight to his seat. It took six men to throw him off the train, seat and all.

In 1845, Frederick published *The Narrative of the Life of Frederick Douglass, an American Slave.* This book revealed the facts he had withheld for four years—his real name and where he was from. The one thing he did not describe was his escape, to protect others who might try to escape the same way.

Narrative was an instant best seller. It was especially popular in the North and steered more people to the antislavery cause. But Frederick was now in even more danger. Though he had many powerful friends who would protect him, that didn't mean a hired searcher couldn't trap him and spirit him away.

Chapter 6
The North Star

The idea of being captured haunted Frederick.
By law, he still belonged to the Aulds. After
making sure that the money from his book
sales would go directly to Anna, Frederick left
the household in her capable hands and fled to
England. There, and in Ireland and Scotland,
he gave speeches in nearly all the large cities and
towns, asking for help ending American slavery.
Already famous in America, Frederick became
well-known in Europe as well.

Frederick was amazed to find that in England,
Black people were treated the same as white people.
Whether on a train or in a restaurant, hotel, or
church, he was welcome without concern for his
color. No one insulted him or threw him out, as they

often did in America. He felt refreshed and, for the first time, truly free. It was tempting to move his family overseas, but Frederick felt he must go home. How else could he help the millions still enslaved?

Then a group of his English friends did something remarkable. They raised money to buy Frederick's freedom from the Aulds. And the Aulds agreed. In exchange for 150 British pounds, or about $700, Hugh Auld signed papers freeing Frederick forever.

Freedom! Now Frederick could devote himself fully to his life's work of ending slavery. After twenty-one months abroad, Frederick returned to America with plans of starting his own antislavery newspaper. He moved his family to Rochester, New York, where there was a strong abolitionist community.

CANADA

LAKE ONTARIO

NEW YORK

Rochester

Seneca Falls

PENNSYLVANIA

NEW JERSEY

Frederick published the first issue of his paper, *The North Star*, in 1847. The paper, named after the star that guided freedom seekers to freedom, published accounts of enslaved people who escaped to freedom and news about successful people who were formerly enslaved. It printed stories and poems by Black writers. It spoke out against the poor treatment of Black people in the North. *The North Star* made Frederick a true leader of his people. In 1851, he would rename the publication *Frederick Douglass' Paper*.

In his newspaper and in his talks, Frederick also spoke up for women's rights. Women could not vote. In most states they could not own property. The few jobs open to them did not pay well. Women were expected to marry, keep house, and raise children while their husbands handled outside affairs. In 1848, America's first Woman's Rights Convention was held in Seneca Falls, New York. Frederick attended the event and supported it in *The North Star.*

A MIGHTY TEAM: SUSAN B. ANTHONY AND ELIZABETH CADY STANTON

SUSAN B. ANTHONY

SUSAN B. ANTHONY AND ELIZABETH CADY STANTON WERE COURAGEOUS, DETERMINED REFORMERS WHO WORKED FOR EQUAL RIGHTS FOR WOMEN. THEY WERE ALSO ACTIVE IN THE ABOLITIONIST MOVEMENT. ANTHONY AND STANTON MET AND BEGAN WORKING TOGETHER IN 1851. IN 1869, THEY FORMED THE NATIONAL WOMAN SUFFRAGE ASSOCIATION TO FOCUS ON WOMEN'S RIGHT TO VOTE. STANTON DRAFTED A VOTING-RIGHTS AMENDMENT TO THE CONSTITUTION THAT WAS FIRST INTRODUCED IN 1878. UNFORTUNATELY, THE AMENDMENT WAS NOT ADOPTED UNTIL 1920, BY WHICH TIME BOTH WOMEN HAD DIED.

ELIZABETH CADY STANTON

Frederick's work as an abolitionist did not stop with his newspaper or speeches. His house in Rochester was also a stop, or "station," on the Underground Railroad. This "railroad" had no tracks or trains. Instead it was a network of people and houses that helped enslaved people escape from the South. As "conductors" on this railroad, Frederick and Anna provided food and shelter to freedom seekers before seeing them off on the last leg of their journey to freedom in Canada.

HARRIET TUBMAN, THE BLACK MOSES

HARRIET TUBMAN WAS BORN ENSLAVED IN MARYLAND AROUND 1820. AS A YOUNG WOMAN, SHE ESCAPED SLAVERY ON THE UNDERGROUND RAILROAD. SHE THEN RISKED HER OWN FREEDOM TO RETURN TO THE SOUTH AGAIN AND AGAIN, HELPING MORE THAN THREE HUNDRED PEOPLE, INCLUDING MEMBERS OF HER FAMILY, REACH FREEDOM IN THE NORTH. AS THE MOST FAMOUS "CONDUCTOR" ON THE UNDERGROUND RAILROAD, HARRIET WAS PROUD TO SAY, "I NEVER RAN MY TRAIN OFF THE TRACK AND I NEVER LOST A PASSENGER."

Frederick's work on the Underground Railroad brought him "unspeakable joy." But helping freedom seekers was risky. He and Anna could be fined up to $1,000 and sent to jail.

Frederick and others began to worry that peaceful means were not enough to achieve their goals. One white man who wanted to use force to end slavery was Frederick's friend and fellow abolitionist John Brown. In 1859, Brown asked Frederick to join him in a raid to steal government weapons at

JOHN BROWN

Harper's Ferry, Virginia. Brown planned to give the weapons to enslaved people so they could fight against the people who were enslaving them. Brown hoped that a mass rebellion would end slavery once and for all. Frederick was sure the plan would fail. He told Brown he would not be part of it.

Brown did secure the weapons from an arsenal in Harper's Ferry, Virginia. But about half of his men were killed, and he and some of the others were captured by US soldiers the next day.

Officials found letters from Frederick in John Brown's carpetbag. Frederick had nothing to do with the raid. However, he knew no one would believe this. With government officials on his tail, Frederick fled to Canada.

From Canada, Frederick left for England, only to return six months later when word came that his youngest child, Annie, had died. Deeply saddened, Frederick took the first steamer home—no matter what danger awaited him. Back in America, he found that to a growing number of people, Brown had become a hero.

The United States was now focused on the presidential election of 1860. Frederick supported Republican Abraham Lincoln, the only candidate who opposed the spread of slavery. Although Frederick did not agree with everything Lincoln stood for, he threw himself into campaigning for him.

ABRAHAM LINCOLN

Chapter 7
War Between the States

Abraham Lincoln won the election. He took office on March 4, 1861. In the six months following the election, fearing Lincoln would end slavery, eleven states in the South seceded, or broke away from, the United States. Together, they formed the Confederate States of America and elected their own president. And on April 12, 1861, Confederate troops attacked a Union garrison at Fort Sumter, South Carolina.

The Civil War had begun.

To Lincoln, the purpose of the war was to defeat the Confederacy and bring the Southern states back into the Union. To Frederick, it was that and more: It was a battle over slavery. Frederick was determined to ensure that if the

CANADA

TERRITORIES

UNION STATES

CONFEDERATE STATES

MEXICO

BORDER STATES

Union won, slavery would be abolished forever.

From the start, Frederick felt strongly that all enslaved people should be freed and allowed to serve in the Union army. This would show Americans that Black people were as brave and deserving of liberty as white people. And with formerly enslaved people fighting for the Union, the South would be drained of its workforce.

Lincoln, however, was slow to act. To achieve his goals, Frederick gave hundreds of speeches, wrote to the country's leaders, and spoke out in his newspaper, which he had renamed *Douglass' Monthly.*

By 1862, with the war still raging, the Union needed more troops. In September, Lincoln issued the Emancipation Proclamation. It freed all enslaved people in Confederate territory on January 1, 1863. The Proclamation also allowed Black people to enlist in the Union army.

It was an amazing milestone. Frederick knew the Emancipation Proclamation wasn't perfect. For one thing, Lincoln didn't really have control over any of the enslaved people in Confederate territory. There were also a million enslaved people in the border states, states that remained in the Union but still allowed slavery. The Proclamation didn't free them. But the Emancipation Proclamation was a turning point in the war and in the fight against slavery.

On January 1, news that the Proclamation had officially been signed came into the Boston church where Frederick waited with three thousand others. The crowd erupted into "shouts of praise . . . sobs and tears" and celebrated long into the night.

Now Frederick could work to recruit Black soldiers. The governor of Massachusetts asked for his help filling the ranks of the Fifty-Fourth Regiment Massachusetts Volunteer Infantry, a regiment of all-Black troops. Frederick wrote a powerful article titled "Men of Color, to Arms!" to rally Black people to fight for freedom. "This is your hour and mine," he wrote. "The iron gate of our prison stands half open." He traveled through the North signing up Black troops. Frederick's sons, Lewis and Charles, were among the first to enlist. In all, nearly two hundred thousand Black soldiers would fight bravely for the Union and help win many battles.

But Frederick was troubled when he found that Black soldiers were not treated the same as white soldiers. Black soldiers received about half the pay of white soldiers. They got little training, were not commissioned as officers, and were not rewarded for bravery. Frederick used his pen and his words, writing letters and speaking out for equal treatment. Then he went to Washington, DC, to request a meeting with President Lincoln. Here was a formerly enslaved person, one who had openly disagreed with the president, hoping to meet with the most powerful man in the nation. How would he be received? Would he be received at all?

At the White House, President Lincoln welcomed Frederick as an equal. He listened carefully to his concerns and agreed that Black soldiers had proved themselves in battle.

Frederick didn't get all the answers he hoped for that day. But he was encouraged by Lincoln's attention and felt the president was a good man. By the end of the war, Black soldiers got equal pay and were allowed to become officers. Some received medals for bravery.

Later in the war, President Lincoln invited
Frederick back to Washington. He asked for his
help designing a plan to evacuate enslaved people
from the South if the Union did not win the war.
Respect between the two men grew.

President Lincoln was reelected in 1864.
After Lincoln's second inauguration in March
1865, Frederick went to the reception at the

White House to congratulate him. No Black American had ever done this, and police tried to keep Frederick out. But when Lincoln saw him, he said boldly, "Here comes my friend Douglass." Lincoln wanted to know what Frederick thought of the speech he'd given that day. "There is no man in the country whose opinion I value more than yours," Lincoln said.

Five weeks later, the Civil War ended with the South surrendering. The Thirteenth Amendment to the Constitution, adopted later that year, abolished slavery forever. What had seemed impossible to young Frederick was now reality. Four million Black people were free. Frederick felt "exceeding joy over these stupendous achievements," especially the abolition of slavery, "which had been the deepest desire and the great labor of my life."

Lincoln now faced the difficult task of reuniting the country. He wanted to "bind up the nation's wounds" and welcome back the Southern states. But this job would be left to others. Five days after the Confederate surrender, President Lincoln was shot and killed by a proslavery actor named John Wilkes Booth.

Frederick shared the nation's shock and sorrow at the loss of their great president—a man he called "so amiable, so kind, humane, and honest,

JOHN WILKES BOOTH

that one is at a loss to know how he could have had an enemy on earth." And although Frederick was overjoyed by the abolition of slavery, he also felt lost. With slavery gone, "my voice was no longer needed," Frederick wrote. "Where should I go, and what should I do?"

Chapter 8
Marshal Douglass

Frederick needn't have worried about what would occupy his time. Invitations poured in for him to speak at lecture halls and colleges. In the late 1860s, lectures provided audiences with a mix of education and entertainment. It was a good job and paid well.

But Frederick was not finished in his quest for equal rights. Although Black people were no longer enslaved, they were not yet fully free. Black people were not citizens. They could not vote. Frederick felt strongly that this newfound freedom wouldn't mean much until Black Americans had a say in government affairs. Frederick spoke out, as always, and supported those in power who shared his views.

In 1868, the Fourteenth Amendment allowed formerly enslaved people to become citizens and granted all citizens the same protection under America's laws. In 1870, the Fifteenth Amendment gave Black men the right to vote. The American Anti-Slavery Society disbanded that year. At its last meeting, Frederick said, "I seem to myself to be living in a new world."

Still, many did not welcome progress for Black people. In 1872, Frederick and Anna's home in Rochester was burned. Deeply saddened, the couple moved to Washington, DC. There, Frederick was asked to run a Black bank, where formerly enslaved people could invest their new savings. The bank had not been doing well, and its owners hoped Frederick's name and image would help bring it around. But the bank collapsed only three months later. Frederick was humiliated.

In 1877, President Hayes appointed Frederick US marshal of the District of Columbia.

RECONSTRUCTION

ANDREW JOHNSON

THE PERIOD AFTER THE CIVIL WAR WAS KNOWN AS RECONSTRUCTION. THE ENORMOUS TASK OF REUNITING NORTH AND SOUTH FELL TO PRESIDENT ANDREW JOHNSON, WHO WAS A SOUTHERNER AND DID NOT SHARE LINCOLN'S VISION.

THERE WERE FOUR MILLION FORMERLY ENSLAVED PEOPLE WITHOUT FOOD, HOMES, OR MONEY. FEW COULD READ OR WRITE. A GOVERNMENT AGENCY CALLED THE FREEDMEN'S BUREAU HELPED PROVIDE BASIC NEEDS AND ESTABLISHED THOUSANDS OF PUBLIC SCHOOLS AND SEVERAL COLLEGES FOR BLACK PEOPLE. SOLDIERS FROM THE NORTH WERE STATIONED IN THE SOUTH TO HELP PROTECT BLACK PEOPLE AND THEIR RIGHTS. BY 1875, SIXTEEN BLACK MEN HAD BEEN ELECTED TO CONGRESS, AND HUNDREDS SERVED IN THEIR STATE LEGISLATURES.

HOWEVER, THE PROGRESS WAS SHORT-LIVED. WHEN RECONSTRUCTION ENDED AND US TROOPS LEFT THE SOUTH IN 1877, MOST OF THE GAINS BLACK PEOPLE HAD MADE DISAPPEARED.

Frederick's post was an honor and a first for a Black man, though he had little power. He and Anna bought a large home overlooking Washington. The house, named Cedar Hill, was an elegant place to welcome friends and family. In 1881,

RUTHERFORD B. HAYES

Frederick published his third autobiography, *The Life and Times of Frederick Douglass.*

(Frederick's second autobiography, *My Bondage and My Freedom*, had been published in 1855.)

Around the time Frederick bought Cedar Hill, a friend invited him back to Saint Michaels, Maryland. Thomas Auld, now in his eighties and very sick, learned Frederick was there and asked him to visit.

Once enslaver and the enslaved person, the two now met as equals. Frederick held Thomas's hand as they spoke freely about the past. Frederick asked what his old enslaver thought of his escape to freedom. "Frederick, I always knew you were too smart to be a slave," Thomas replied, "and had I been in your place, I should have done as you did." The two parted on good terms. Thomas died soon after.

JAMES A. GARFIELD

In 1882, Anna died. The family missed her terribly. Frederick was lonely, and after more than a year without Anna, he thought about remarrying. The previous year, President James A. Garfield had appointed Frederick recorder of deeds for the District of Columbia.

In that position, Frederick hired a clerk named Helen Pitts. Helen believed in equal rights and in votes for women. She and Frederick had much in common. They fell in love, and in 1884 they married.

HELEN PITTS

Frederick and Helen were happy, but many others were outraged. Helen was twenty years younger than Frederick, and she was white. Even Frederick's children were upset. But Frederick saw no problem with the union. He said his first wife was Black, like his mother, and his second wife was white, like his father. Together, Frederick and Helen toured Europe. From 1889 to 1891 they lived in Haiti, where Frederick served as US minister and consul general.

Between and after his travels, Frederick continued to speak out for equal rights and against the violence Black people experienced in the South. He was growing tired. Still, he fought for liberty until the very end. On February 20, 1895, after attending a women's rights meeting, Frederick had a heart attack and died. He was seventy-seven.

THE CIVIL RIGHTS ACT OF 1964 AND THE VOTING RIGHTS ACT OF 1965

FOR DECADES AFTER RECONSTRUCTION, BLACK PEOPLE IN THE SOUTH WERE FORCED TO EAT IN SEPARATE RESTAURANTS, LEARN IN SEPARATE SCHOOLS, AND RIDE IN THE BACKS OF PUBLIC BUSES. THEY WERE KEPT FROM VOTING BY LITERACY TESTS, POLL TAXES (FEES CHARGED FOR VOTING), AND VIOLENCE.

IN 1964, PRESIDENT LYNDON JOHNSON SIGNED THE CIVIL RIGHTS ACT TO GUARANTEE BLACK

PEOPLE FAIR TREATMENT IN PUBLIC PLACES AND
IN JOBS. THE FOLLOWING YEAR, THE VOTING
RIGHTS ACT OF 1965 ENFORCED THE FIFTEENTH
AMENDMENT, BANNING LITERACY TESTS AND OTHER
REQUIREMENTS THAT KEPT CITIZENS FROM VOTING
BECAUSE OF THE COLOR OF THEIR SKIN. AS
FREDERICK DOUGLASS HAD SAID ONE HUNDRED
YEARS BEFORE, BLACK PEOPLE WERE NOT REALLY
FREE IF THEY COULD NOT VOTE.

The nation had lost its most famous and ardent Black leader. Black schools in Washington closed for his funeral. Thousands passed by his casket to pay their respects at Metropolitan AME Church in Washington and then at City Hall in Rochester.

Statues and monuments would be built in Rochester, New York City, and Baltimore. Schools, roads, and bridges have been named in his honor.

With his courage to do and say things no Black man had done before, Frederick Douglass broke barriers between the races and inspired other civil rights activists. He will always be remembered for his passionate work to make America a better place—one that lives up to the ideals it was founded upon and guarantees freedom for all.

FREDERICK DOUGLASS
1818 – 1895

TIMELINE OF
FREDERICK DOUGLASS'S LIFE

1818	Frederick Augustus Washington Bailey is born
1824	Frederick goes to work at the home of Aaron Anthony, the man who enslaved him
1826	Frederick is sent to work for Hugh Auld in the city of Baltimore
1831	Frederick buys his first book, *The Columbian Orator*
1834	Thomas Auld, the next person who enslaved Frederick, hires him out to an enslaver named Edward Covey
1836	Attempts to escape but is put in jail; returns to Hugh Auld
1838	Escapes dressed as a sailor and changes his name to Frederick Douglass. Marries Anna Murray and moves to Massachusetts
1841	Speaks at Massachusetts Anti-Slavery Society convention
1845	Publishes *Narrative of the Life of Frederick Douglass*, then goes to England for safety
1846	British friends raise money to purchase Frederick's freedom
1847	Moves to Rochester, New York, and starts his own paper, *The North Star*
1848	Speaks at Woman's Rights Convention in Seneca Falls
1855	Publishes his second autobiography, *My Bondage and My Freedom*
1860	Campaigns for presidential candidate Abraham Lincoln
1863	Recruits Black soldiers for the Union
1868	Campaigns for presidential candidate Ulysses S. Grant
1877	Appointed US marshal of the District of Columbia
1881	Publishes third autobiography, *The Life and Times of Frederick Douglass*
1884	Marries second wife, Helen Pitts
1889	Appointed US minister to Haiti
1895	Frederick dies of a heart attack on February 20

TIMELINE OF THE WORLD

The Missouri Compromise admits Missouri as a state that allows slavery and Maine as a free state	1820
The Erie Canal is completed in New York	1825
Nat Turner, an enslaved man, leads a revolt in Virginia	1831
Hans Christian Andersen publishes first book of fairy tales	1835
The siege at the Alamo in San Antonio, Texas	1836
The first covered wagons travel westward	1841
Samuel F.B. Morse demonstrates the telegraph	1844
Potato famine in Ireland	1845
California gold rush begins	1848
Congress passes the Fugitive Slave Law	1850
US Supreme Court rules that enslaved people are not citizens	1857
Charles Darwin publishes *On the Origin of Species*	1859
US Civil War begins	1861
Emancipation Proclamation takes effect	1863
US Civil War ends	1865
Transcontinental railroad connects the United States from east to west	1869
Alexander Graham Bell invents the telephone	1876
Clara Barton founds the American Red Cross	1881
Mark Twain publishes *The Adventures of Huckleberry Finn*	1884
The first skyscraper, the ten-story Home Insurance Building in Chicago, is completed	1885
The Statue of Liberty is dedicated in New York Harbor	1886

BIBLIOGRAPHY

Douglass, Frederick. **My Bondage and My Freedom**. New York: Miller, Orton & Mulligan, 1855.

Douglass, Frederick. **Narrative of the Life of Frederick Douglass, an American Slave**. Boston: The Anti-Slavery Office, 1845.

Douglass, Frederick. **The Life and Times of Frederick Douglass**. Boston: De Wolfe, Fiske, 1892.

* Freedman, Russell. **Abraham Lincoln and Frederick Douglass: The Story Behind an American Friendship**. Boston: Clarion Books, 2012.

* McCurdy, Michael. **Escape from Slavery: The Boyhood of Frederick Douglass in His Own Words**. New York: Alfred A. Knopf, 1994.

McFeely, William S. **Frederick Douglass**. New York: Norton, 1991.

Quarles, Benjamin. **Frederick Douglass**. New York: Atheneum, 1968.

* Ruffin, Frances E. **Frederick Douglass: Rising Up from Slavery**. New York: Sterling Publishing, 2008.

* Sanders, Nancy. **Frederick Douglass for Kids**. Chicago: Chicago Review Press, 2012.

* Books for young readers

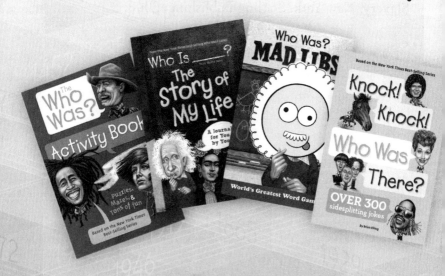